Great W Branch Lines

A Pictorial Survey

Compiled by
C.W. Judge

THE OAKWOOD PRESS

Typeset by Oakwood Graphics.
Repro by Ford Graphics, Ringwood, Hants.
Printed by The Witney Press, Witney, Oxon.

Acknowledgements

My thanks go to the people who over the last few years have supplied many prints for selection in this book. Particularly John Smith of Lens of Sutton, H.C. Casserley's son, Richard, J.R. Morten, J.S. Kite, Douglas Thompson, Roger Kidner, John Alsop, Neville Bridger and Warwick Burton the custodian of the Mowat Collection.

Above: A typical Great Western branch line scene. The summer of May 1932 with a Totnes to Ashburton train leaving Buckfastleigh and crossing the River Dart, auto-coach No. 32 being propelled by a class '517' 0-4-2T. *E.R. Morten*

Front cover Two commercial colour postcards. (*Top*) The terminus at Malmesbury with Malmesbury Abbey in the distance. (*Bottom*) Trawsfynydd station on the Blaenau Festiniog branch. *(Both) John Alsop Collection*

Rear cover: A GWR poster promoting the delights of Looe in Cornwall.
South Devon Railway Trust

Published by
The Oakwood Press
P.O. Box 13, Usk, Mon., NP5 1YS.

Contents

A GWR steam railcar seen here leaving Paddington. These vehicles proved very useful and were introduced in 1903, two initially being built to a Churchward design, 57 ft long with 52 seats and put to work on the Stroud Valley service. By October 1906, 80 steam cars were in use.
Author's Collection

This 0-4-2T, No. 5806, was one of 20 such locomotives built by the Great Western Railway at its Swindon Works in 1933 and commonly used on branch lines where push-pull working was not required (not being fitted for this), appearing virtually anywhere around the GWR system.
Author's Collection

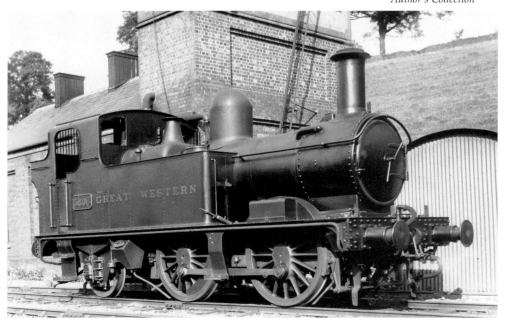

Introduction

Why another photographic Great Western branch line book you may ask? The answer is that many GWR branch line photographs appear in specialist books which cover the branch in minute detail. This is useful for the local historian or modeller but means that good and interesting photographs of branches are for the eyes of a relatively few only; hence this small inexpensive book has been compiled covering many branches.

This book does not therefore set out to be a history or even cover all of the GWR system, but instead it is intended to capture the scenes of days long gone on, I believe, one of the most evocative railways that ever existed. All the views are taken before the 1948 Nationalisation and therefore are 'truly Great Western', a few have been seen before in 'more expensive books', but have been included here to tell a fuller story.

These GWR branch lines were very important and can be compared with the function of the arms and legs of the human body. These 'limbs' or branch lines supplied the main GWR system with passengers and freight to keep the whole system profitable and working; something Beeching never did grasp!

The photographs are laid out in approximate geographic sequence starting from London, heading west towards the West Country, then returning towards Wales, the border country and the West Midlands. To define a branch line is almost impossible and I hope that the reader will forgive several choices which might appear 'marginal'. The three photographs included with this introduction give an indication of the basic type of motive power developed over the years by the GWR to help sustain branch line traffic.

I hope that the 136 photographs in this book bring back fond memories of holidays taken by rail or, for the younger reader, help them understand the complex network of rural branch lines that the GWR established in the heyday of rail travel. Perhaps also the photographs will help the GWR modeller with some small detail to make their model more authentic and prove a valuable addition to your railway library.

C.W. Judge
1998

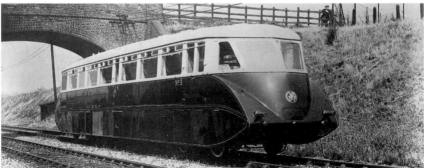

Nicknamed 'The Flying Banana', these vehicles were designed at Swindon and introduced in 1933. Being oil engines, this was the first time that the GWR had not been reliant on coal. Easy to service and even easier and cleaner to operate, they soon became popular with crews. Here we see the forerunner of the diesel multiple unit, which became the mainstay of British Railways. *Author's Collection*

Colnbrook Station

The Staines branch left the main line at West Drayton & Yiewsley which was just a few miles out of the Capital. It curved away north, a short distance from the station there was a junction where a branch to Uxbridge continued northwards, and then swung due south on a tight curve passing under the main line. The first station reached was Colnbrook (seen here in 1921) which was the original terminus of the branch, opened in August 1884. This station contained two platforms and was used as a passing point for branch services. The style of the station buildings and station master's house is somewhat unusual. Colnbrook signal box was provided c. 1904.

Lens of Sutton

A view of the platform at Staines with a typical service on the branch in 1935. A pannier tank locomotive is in charge of the auto-coach No. 33. Note the milk churns and unusual canopy front weatherboard design.   *Lens of Sutton*

The terminus building at Staines was converted from a private house and opened in November 1885. This saved over £1,150 in the construction costs; it is seen here on a wet May day in 1933.
                    Lens of Sutton

Uxbridge had the privilege of two GWR branch lines. This view shows Cowley station (the only intermediate station) on the Uxbridge (Vine Street) to West Drayton branch of 2½ miles length, opened in September 1856. This was a substantial station for a branch line with a double track and was rebuilt in 1904 when this photograph was taken. On the up side platform there were brick buildings which contained a booking office and hall, general waiting room, ladies' and gents' toilets with a smaller brick shelter on the down platform. The branch handled over 50,000 passengers in 1923 so was of considerable importance to the GWR.   *Lens of Sutton*

The other branch serving Uxbridge originated at Denham on the Paddington to Birmingham main line. This branch was opened in May 1907 and the passenger service was withdrawn in September 1939 (also being closed in 1917-1919 as a wartime economy measure). GWR railmotors bore the brunt of the service which, when reopened in 1919, consisted of 12 trains per day. The view below shows the station terminus (buffers on the right) built on wooden piles with a slatted wooden platform. Towards the buffers brick piles have been used with lock-up garages between. The exit was down to the road level through the timber tunnel seen on the right. The station boasted a bicycle lock-up, oil store, booking office, ladies' and gents' facilities and a general waiting room. Note the low level goods siding on the left. *Pat Garland Collection*

A view of Marlow station in Buckinghamshire taken from the buffer stops in 1910. Originally it was opened as Great Marlow but was renamed Marlow in February 1899 and remains operational today. The lower photograph, taken on 4th June, 1915 shows soldiers of the 3rd Battalion Grenadier Guards setting out for their march to Bovingdon Green Camp having arrived in a special train. Several wartime army exercises were conducted on this branch involving movements of men, horses and equipment to test the arrangements (another branch so used being the Faringdon branch in Oxfordshire). *(Both) Lens of Sutton*

An early view of the station approach (*above*) at Henley-on-Thames station (opened 1857) with horse carriages awaiting their passengers. The three-platform station had each of its platforms covered with an overall roof for about 100 feet and the two main platforms had a further 200 ft canopy as can be seen in the lower photograph. For a branch only 4½ miles long, the terminus was very well equipped with a spacious concourse, housing a bookstall, station master's office, general waiting rooms, ticket office, porters' office, parcel office etc. The track layout included seven carriage sidings, over 200 ft of goods sidings, and engine shed and turntable, goods shed with 10 ton crane and a handsome water tower. The signal box contained over 65 levers. Several services from Henley were through trains to Paddington.   *Lens of Sutton and LGRP*

An unusual view from the buffer stops at Watlington station in Oxfordshire *c*. 1900, terminus of the Princes Risborough to Watlington branch, showing the single-road engine shed that was destroyed by fire in 1906. The station building still stands today but in a dilapidated state. The preserved Chinnor & Princes Risborough Railway now operates on part of the branch from Princes Risborough to Chinnor. *Below*: Shows a similar view but taken on 17th June, 1939 capturing the arrival of the 10.14 am branch service from Princes Risborough. Note the unusual corrugated iron carriage shed on the right, alongside the class '2021' 0-6-0T No. 2055, which regularly worked the branch coupled to an auto-coach.   *Author's Collection and H.C. Casserley*

Bledlow Bridge Halt, on the Watlington branch, looking towards Princes Risborough in 1919. This halt was opened in 1906 and served the small hamlet nearby and is now a part of the Chinnor & Princes Risborough preserved railway route.   *LGRP*

A 1934 view of Chinnor station in GWR days looking towards Watlington. The station building was demolished and the platform broken up in early 1970 but the line continued in railway use until December 1989, when a class '47' diesel with 35 hopper wagons made a final journey into the cement works just beyond the station site. The site has now been transformed with a new platform and is the home of the C&PR Preservation Society which is reinstating the station building to its former glory.   *Author's Collection*

A final view on the Watlington branch as a lonely passenger waits at Lewknor Bridge Halt (built 1906) photographed in 1919. This view shows the original wooden bridge over Sheepcote Lane and notice how well lit the platform was considering the very rural area in which it was situated.
LGRP

An early view from the road bridge of the station at Thame on the Oxford to Princes Risborough branch in Oxfordshire. Retaining its overall roof from opening in August 1862 until the end of passenger service in January 1963, it was the largest station on the 21 mile-long branch. Note the large goods shed and gas lighting around the yard and station area. The lattice girder post signal was unusual for GWR stations. *Author's Collection*

Abingdon station in Oxfordshire was originally constructed as a broad gauge single line of 2½ miles by the Abingdon Railway Co. from a point on the main Oxford to Didcot line near Nuneham. Always worked by the GWR from 1856, it was extended to run alongside the main line to reach Radley station in 1873. The station supported a large goods shed, engine shed and private siding all controlled by a small signal box (opened in 1882). The original building had an overall roof, as can be seen in the lower view. The top view shows the result of a runaway goods train early on the morning of 22nd April, 1908, which smashed into the four empty coaches waiting in the platform road. Abingdon hoped that this crash might provide them with a new station and this proved to be the case when, at a cost of £2,210, a new station was built in 1909.   *(Both) Lens of Sutton*

A rare photograph taken in August 1935 showing '517' class 0-4-2T No. 1159, deputising for the regular engine *Fair Rosamund* which was undergoing overhaul, entering Woodstock station, the terminus of the branch from Kidlington, which closed to all traffic in 1954.   *R.W. Kidner*

The country terminus of Faringdon in Oxfordshire was just 3 miles 41 chains from Uffington, its junction with the Paddington-Bristol main line. First opened on 1st June, 1864 the line served the village for 99 years with closures for passengers in 1951 and freight in 1963. The signal box was a covered ground frame containing six levers and operated by the locomotive crew. The building on the right was the engine shed and the yard to the left (behind the station buildings) contained a goods shed and cattle pens with a loading dock.   *LGRP*

Wallingford Station

A modeller's delight. The 2¾ mile branch to Wallingford was opened in July 1866 from the GWR main line at Wallingford Road (later Cholsey & Moulsford) and closed to passenger traffic in 1959. A very compact layout as can be seen, with the gas works siding on the left and engine shed beyond it. The goods shed and sidings are out of sight to the right of the platform, at the Cholsey end, which was also the location of the signal box.

Lens of Sutton

The 3.21 p.m. entering Basingstoke. G.W.Ry.

Author's Collection

The 3.21 pm service from Reading entering the GWR Basingstoke station terminus with an unidentified 'Bulldog' class locomotive in charge. The lines diverging to the right were the through running lines onto the LSWR main line to Southampton and beyond. The two-track and bay platform terminus had an overall roof, engine and goods shed and was opened in 1848. However in 1932 all GWR trains were directed into the SR station and the old station was then only used for freight.

The GWR absorbed the 47¾ miles of the Didcot, Newbury and Southampton Railway in 1923 and thus it became one of their branch lines (although running on through via Shawford Junction to Southampton) with Winchester (Chesil) the end of the GWR section. Here on 20th May, 1935, No. 3266 is about to leave Winchester (Chesil) for Southampton with one of the four passenger trains operating at that time from Didcot. The GWR installed new electric signalling and point operation here when they took over and just beyond the tunnel seen in this photograph was a single road engine shed with a turntable, being a sub-shed to Didcot.

H.C. Casserley

A 1919 view of Lichfield station, one of the intermediate stations on the DN&SR. The double track through the station was used as a passing loop and the yard had a headshunt, goods shed and cattle pens. The station saw extensive traffic during World War II as the line was a direct route to Southampton from the Midlands. *LGRP*

Highworth in Wiltshire opened in May 1883, the branch terminus was 6½ miles from Swindon. The branch itself had three intermediate stations; Stratton, Stanton, and Hannington and when first opened boasted five trains a day in each direction. Although the passenger service was withdrawn in March 1953, a train was provided both morning and evening for local people working at Swindon GWR Works. Highworth was built on a sharp curve making it very suitable to model due to the fact it would fit into the corner of a room. The top view looks towards Swindon and shows extensive goods stock in the single siding available, which also acted as a headshunt for the goods shed. The lower view, looking towards the buffers shows the ground frame on the platform next to the station building with a good crowd waiting to board the 'local'.   *Brunel University: Mowat/Locomotive Collection and Lens of Sutton*

Stanton was a little-known intermediate station on the Highworth branch in Wiltshire. As can be seen in this 1930 view the facilities were very basic, but doubtless sufficed for the small, rural community. The inevitable milk churns are on the platform together with a solitary seat for waiting passengers. There was a short siding behind the platform (until 1925 there had been two) and a loading gauge may be seen opposite the platform end. The photographer is standing on the level crossing which crossed the line here. On the building end wall, to the right of the gas lamp post is a poster advertising 'Isle of Man TT' races week.

Brunel University; Movat/Locomotive Collection

The Fairford branch in Oxfordshire was opened in two stages, the first from Yarnton Junction to Witney in November 1861 whilst the extension to Fairford itself opened on 15th June, 1873. The terminus station at Fairford was really situated in the middle of nowhere and it was presumed the line would be extended to Cheltenham, this therefore gave the track at Fairford a somewhat long and drawn-out layout. The photograph is an official GWR picture taken in July 1890 when they acquired the line and shows well the station, then the goods shed, sidings, and right in the distance, the water tower and engine shed. *Below*: one of the intermediate stations on the branch was Kelmscott & Langford (officially Platform) opened in 1907 and consisting of just one platform with a pagoda-style building and a goods siding. This photograph was taken just after the opening and shows the local carpenters who had worked on the project.   *(Both) Author's Collection*

Lechlade, a pretty intermediate station on the Fairford branch in Oxfordshire, is seen in 1946. From the state of the gardens, both on the platform and those on the lineside beyond the point rodding and signal wires, the staff boasted some keen gardeners. Despite the presence of the signal box, which had opened in 1893, this only controlled siding connections, as there was no passing loop here.

Brunel University: Mowat/Locomotive Collection

Devizes station in Wiltshire looking towards Holt from the tunnel end, in the 1930s. This station had an overall roof when opened in 1857 as a branch terminus. A further five years elapsed before the line was opened through to Hungerford (through a 190 yds-long tunnel). With three platforms, goods shed and loading shed, this was a busy station. *Douglas Thompson*

Chippenham was the junction for the Calne branch, which is chiefly remembered for its conveyance of the products of Messrs Harris of Calne, the pork pie makers. The line did not survive long in the Beeching era, closing completely in 1965. In this view a branch train has just arrived from Calne comprising a steam railmotor and auto-coach, and is standing at the down main line platform. The line in the middle of this view had buffer stops placed in its length and the far (east) end acted as a branch bay for Calne. *Douglas Thompson*

Calne station in Wiltshire was the terminus of the 5 mile 24 chains branch from Chippenham. It was a busy and important branch as it had eight large sidings to meet the needs of Harris's factory and also three very large RAF training camps in the area. In 1959 for instance, 98,000 passengers bought tickets, with over 200,000 using the station, 24,000 tons of freight and 17,000 parcels were handled. The layout consisted of a large goods shed and double-sided loading dock. The signal box and water tower were situated on the platform but no engine shed was provided. The top view, looking towards Chippenham, shows the high level of staff for a branch line station in 1912 (dates are on the posters). The GWR motor-bus has the destination of Calne in the window and would have probably connected with the Marlborough service.   *(Both) Lens of Sutton*

This view of Marlborough High Level (*c.* 1930) gives an impression of the cramped station site, the picture probably taken while the branch goods was carrying out shunting operations (note that the brake van left is branded 'Marlborough'). The engine shed can be seen in the distance (*centre*). For economy reasons, the GWR closed its own branch line in 1933 and diverted trains from Savernake onto the former Midland & South Western Junction Railway route (which can be seen behind the fenceposts, *right*) into the adjacent Marlborough Low Level station. The High Level site was retained for goods traffic only. In the view below motor-bus No. AF 64, a 20 hp Milnes-Daimler owned by the GWR is seen standing at Marlborough station. This bus operated between Marlborough and Calne, both termini of GWR branch lines. Little did the GWR realise when they introduced these services and vehicles that they would gradually replace the trains and it was in the long term a self-destructive move.

Brunel University: Mowat/Locomotive Collection and British Rail

An evocative view taken on 23rd May, 1929 of the GWR Marlborough High Level station's engine shed, with 'Metro' 2-4-0 tank No. 1499 simmering in the sun. This locomotive was officially allocated to this shed which was closed (as was the station) early in 1933. The high, cast-iron, ornate water tower dates from 1879 and had a 9,600 gallon capacity in its 28 ft x 10 ft x 6 ft deep tank. The shed was of broad gauge construction similar to Malmesbury, being 69 ft long by 19 ft wide and contained a 39 ft inspection pit.

H.C. Casserley

The Malmesbury branch in Wiltshire was 6 miles 4 furlongs in length from the junction station at Dauntsey on the Bristol line. This 1932 view of Malmesbury looking from the buffer stops towards Great Somerford (the only intermediate station on the branch) shows the single road engine shed which was opened in 1871 and closed in 1951, and still survives today! The ruins of the Norman Malmesbury Abbey can clearly be seen over the station canopy, dominating the scene. The black structure on the right was a coal bunker for station use.

Mowat Collection/W.R. Burton

An unidentified class '517' 0-4-2T waits to depart from Malmesbury in 1932 with two milk vans coupled into a normal branch train. The branch was shortened by a new spur being constructed at Little Somerford in 1933 into the main line from Wootton Bassett to South Wales. However the old line to Great Somerford was used for storage until the 1950s. *Lens of Sutton*

Saddle tank 0-6-0 No. 1952 stands at the engine shed entrance on the left, in this pre-1900 view of Cirencester station approach. Opened in May 1841 as Cirencester, it was renamed Cirencester Town in July 1924. The branch was only 4 miles 17 chains long from its junction station at Kemble. This superb official GWR photograph contains a wealth of information for the modeller: note the very large goods shed that dominated the yard and the unusual lattice post signals in the distance.

British Rail

During 1910/1911 the station at Lambourn (Berkshire) was rebuilt by the GWR in brick to replace the wooden construction which had originally been erected by the Lambourn Valley Railway in 1897. The GWR acquired the railway on 1st July, 1905. In 1937 the locomotive shed was closed with the introduction of the GWR diesel railcars. These railcars were found to be able to pull horse boxes (racehorse training being the main industry in the area) and so virtually took over the branch services. *Lens of Sutton*

At the end of a branch from Westbury was Salisbury (GWR) and here was situated a substantial stone-built running shed originally built in 1856 for the broad gauge. This interesting view was captured by an official GWR photographer in 1899 to record the old shed before a new one was constructed. *British Rail*

A corner of Weymouth Town station, seen in 1931. The picture is full of interest - the licensed porters (Nos. 8 and 28), who doubtless hurried your luggage to the town's hotels or quay, pose with their trolleys for the camera. A private bus for the Royal Hotel stands at the entrance. Even the dog is interested in the cameraman. In particular, notice how clean and tidy everything is - not a piece of litter to be seen anywhere!

British Rail

Weymouth Tramway and Weymouth Quay station with a train of clerestory stock in the platform.
Commercial postcard

A goods working sets off from Weymouth Quay to Weymouth Junction in June 1934, hauled by an ex-Whitland & Cardigan Railway 0-6-0T, numbered 1331 by the GWR. This engine worked the tramway between 1928 and 1935. As well as its whistle it has a special bell for working over the Tramway. Notice the shunter sitting comfortably on the footplate. One wonders if the little boy *really* wanted to wear that hat!
E.R. Morten

Abbotsbury station, the terminus of the 8¼ mile branch from Weymouth, seen here around 1907 with station master Henry Weston centre stage. One of the posters announces the opening of the new Castle Cary to Langport cut-off line in 1906. The station boasted a goods shed, engine shed and cattle dock with a 11-lever signal box when opened on 9th November, 1885. Local stone was used for the building to the design by the GWR architect William Clarke. The branch closed to all traffic in December 1952. *Lens of Sutton*

The main station building at Bridport station in Dorset, with the train standing in the up platform, looking towards Maiden Newton which was the junction for the branch on the Weymouth main line. Built by the Bridport Railway and opened on 12th November, 1857, the branch was absorbed by the GWR in 1901. The unusual feature of the station was that the signal box, goods shed and main buildings were all in a straight line whereas the platform contained an acute curve indicating that the station was at one time a terminus. This photograph shows this layout as well as members of the station staff. *Lens of Sutton*

Although Ilminster was the principal intermediate station on the Taunton-Chard branch, like all the others it only had one platform and the crossing loop could only be used by freight trains. *Above*: The station staff pose for their photograph. In the view below there is a good variety of rolling stock on display including a number of milk vans (Siphons) opposite the signal box as this was an important centre for dairy products. Both of these delightful pictures were taken *c.* 1930.   *(Both) Brunel University: Mowat/Locomotive Collection*

Locomotive No. 4555, a '45XX' class 2-6-2T leaves Yeovil Town station with a two-coach local service on 21st May, 1935, *en route* to Castle Cary. The road bridge in the distance spans three tracks with the two on the left curving away to Yeovil Junction. The GWR had its principal station at Yeovil Pen Mill (which will be the next stop for this service) but had exchange sidings at this joint SR/GWR station.   *H.C. Casserley*

Clifton Maybank (Goods) was the terminus of a very short freight branch which ran from Clifton Maybank Junction on the Yeovil-Weymouth GWR line and terminated alongside Yeovil Junction station on the LSWR (later SR) main line from Waterloo to Exeter and beyond. An interchange siding allowed for transfer of traffic between the companies. Here an unidentified pannier tank is carrying out shunting in 1933. The branch closed in 1937, after which goods transfers took place via Yeovil Town.   *Brunel University: Mowat/Locomotive Collection*

Hatch, on the Taunton-Chard branch, looking towards Hatch tunnel (152 yds) and Taunton. There is only one platform here, the loop on the right being only for goods trains. Although indistinct in the photograph the running signals are pulled 'off' in either direction, the signal box (*right*) was switched out at the time the picture was taken, *c.* 1930. The small goods yard appears to be well used.   *Brunel University: Mowat/Locomotive Collection*

Chard station had in its early days two station masters, staff and two signal boxes as it was a shared station between the LSWR and B&ER (later the GWR). The platform seen in the photograph was a mixed gauge interchange platform between broad and standard gauges and the turntable supported both types of track! This 1930s view captures well the substantial ornate overall roof at this station. Passenger services ceased in September 1962.   *Lens of Sutton*

A delightful view of Hemyock station in Devon, the end of the branch line from Tiverton Junction. Opened in May 1876 and closed to passengers on 9th September, 1963 it however operated for many years more, catering for the large milk output from the dairy situated at the end of the branch. Here No. 1300, a 2-4-0T built by Ince Forge in 1878 (but finished at Swindon Works) for the South Devon Railway and named *Mercury*, has drawn the 12.50 pm service from Tiverton Jn, run-round its train and re-assembled the formation for the 2.45 pm to Tiverton Jn on 25th May, 1929. The coach is ex-Manchester & Milford Railway stock.   *H.C. Casserley*

Looking over the fence from Victoria Road, the main wooden station buildings at Barnstaple (Victoria Road) can be viewed with a train having just arrived. Note the gas tank wagon in the centre road. The station opened as just 'Barnstaple' in November 1873 being constructed as broad gauge. It was converted in May 1881 to standard gauge and the name Victoria Road added in 1950. A spacious and comprehensive layout with many sidings, goods shed and engine shed (closed January 1951) served this station until closure to passengers on 13th June, 1960, after which trains from Taunton were diverted to the SR Barnstaple Junction station over the East Curve, avoiding Victoria Road, which had been closed since 1939. The Barnstaple branch closed on 3rd October, 1966.   *Lens of Sutton*

The Exe Valley Railway in Devon ran from Exeter to Dulverton, some 24¾ miles. Ten miles from Exeter was situated Cadeleigh and Bickleigh station (renamed Cadeleigh in May 1906) and opened in May 1885. The Exe Valley line was finally closed on 7th October, 1963. Note the cattle pens (this short spur was removed by 1898) leading to a 'through' goods shed and the gas tank wagon on the back of the four-wheeled passenger stock on the train in the station. *Below*: Set in beautiful surroundings on the Exe Valley line is the delightful station of Bampton, which was opened in August 1884 and closed on 7th October, 1963. The station staff appear to have gathered for their photograph in this 1920s view. A line went round the back of the goods shed to a road stone works whilst the cattle pens and signal box were on the right of the photograph opposite the goods shed. Passengers had to cross the road bridge and down a steep track to use the right-hand platform and waiting shelter.   *(Both) Lens of Sutton*

Situated on the very long 44¾ mile Taunton to Barnstaple branch was the important intermediate station of Dulverton. As can be seen in this 1911 view the station was busy with 12 station staff in view, traffic and cycles being man-handled across the lines and plenty of passengers as well for the down service. There is a locomotive working in the yard on the right whilst a further yard appears on the left. It was opened on 1st November, 1873 and closed to passengers on 3rd October, 1966. The earlier station had only two running lines, however the station was extended in 1911 to make an island platform to accommodate the Exe Valley services. The spur line bottom left led to the horse loading dock. The signal box (new in 1910) is on the up platform, just beyond the footbridge, with the large goods shed behind it. The small building by the foot crossing is probably an earlier signal box, now in use as a lamp hut or something similar.

Lens of Sutton

Moretonhampstead in Devon was served by a 12¼ mile branch from Newton Abbot. Here we see a train arriving in 1904 with mixed stock comprising four- and six-wheeled coaches. The station opened in 1866 and is again ideal for railway modelling with its overall roof covering the running lines, a large goods shed with a signal box alongside the engine shed (out of sight). In the early days motor-buses were kept in the building just behind the station for the numerous services into the beautiful surrounding countryside. The service around this time consisted of nine trains each way on weekdays.   *Lens of Sutton*

One of the busy intermediate stations on the branch was Bovey some six miles from Newton Abbot and here a 1920s scene shows the assortment of GWR buses and charabancs in the station yard awaiting the arrival of the connecting train service. These vehicles conveyed tourists to local beauty spots such as Haytor Rocks, The Becky Falls etc.   *Lens of Sutton*

The station at Heathfield, on the Moretonhampstead branch, was the junction for Chudleigh and Trusham (seen coming in from the right beyond the signal box). The line to the left was a private siding into Candy & Co. Pottery Works. Originally named Chudleigh Road, it was re-named Heathfield in October 1882. This station was the interchange between the broad gauge line to Moretonhampstead and the standard gauge Teign Valley line for over 10 years, without any physical connection, and a direct junction between the two lines was not opened until 1916. *Below*: the station of Trusham on the picturesque 17 mile Teign Valley line from Heathfield to Exeter was the third stopping place out of Heathfield *en route* to Exeter. In this 1905 view, an unidentified 0-4-2T of the '517' class hauls four 4-wheeled coaches into the single line platform. Later this station had a passing loop added.   *LGRP and Lens of Sutton*

Churston station on the GWR line to Kingswear was the junction for the 2 mile Brixham branc. The branch bay platform can be seen on the left Opened in 1868 by the Torbay & Brixham Railway Co., it was absorbed by the GWR in 1883.   *Lens of Sutton*

A general view of the branch terminus at Brixham which was situated on a hillside away from the town and not at all convenient for passengers. Taken around 1910 it shows the (1905) station canopy and a very busy scene with plenty of goods wagons in the yard. The branch closed in May 1963 and now the trackbed is a walkway for most of its length.   *Lens of Sutton*

Travelling down from Churston, the terminus of Kingswear is reached. Although served by 'King' class locomotives, this had the quality of a branch line terminus. No. 2182 (later renumbered 4521 in December 1912), built in 1909, shunts alongside the small single road engine shed which closed in 1924, with a saddle tank in the distance.   *Author's Collection*

Just before Kingswear was reached the railway crossed the road at Britannia Crossing, where there was a halt used mainly by workers at the adjacent shipyard of Messrs Philip & Son. In this picture the halt, left of the roadway, obscures the ground frame, called Steam Ferry Crossing, which worked the gates. The ferry, known as the higher ferry, linked the two banks of the river without the need to go through Kingswear. The brake van of an up freight train may just be seen on the left edge of the picture; the distant signal beside it is the Kingswear down (fixed) distant.

C.R. Potts Collection

Dartmouth station was a curiosity as it had no tracks or trains running into it, only boats! Built in 1889, it looked like a GWR station and was the terminal for the railway ferry boats plying passengers across the river to Kingswear.   *Lens of Sutton*

Kingsbridge station was opened in December 1893. The station area and platform were all constructed on a sweeping curve. This photograph was taken on a rainy day in August 1945 and shows No. 5557 with the 11.00 am service to Brent. Note the corrugated carriage shed on the left and the single road engine shed and water tower on the right. Kingsbridge station also served Salcombe Regis and local hotels.   *Lens of Sutton*

The Ashburton branch in Devon was opened in May 1872 as a broad gauge line joining the main South Devon Railway at Totnes, which had been in operation since May 1848. The terminus station of Ashburton was a modeller's joy as it had an overall roof over the two tracks, with one platform being used for passengers and the other being used for cattle with pens alongside. Note the goods shed alongside the platform. Here 0-4-2T No. 4870 waits on 30th August, 1945 with auto-coach No. 96 for its 9½ mile trip along the valley of the River Dart to Totnes.

H.C. Casserley.

The most important intermediate station on the branch was Buckfastleigh (just 2½ miles from the terminus) and here this turn-of-the-century view captures a three-coach train of four-wheeled stock arriving from Ashburton. The branch was converted into standard gauge in May 1892 and officially absorbed into the GWR in 1897. The station had extensive facilities and again the goods shed is alongside the platform. This station survives today and is the home of the (preserved) South Devon Railway Company; the line having been closed in 1958 to passengers it was re-opened on 21st May, 1969 by none other than Dr Beeching!

Lens of Sutton

Opened in January 1898, the Plymstock to Yealmpton branch had five intermediate stations along its 6½ mile length and the top view shows the GWR bus at Yealmpton awaiting its passengers for Modbury and Bigbury-on-Sea. Passenger services closed in 1930, re-opening briefly from 1941 to 1947 and freight lasted until February 1960. The lower view shows an unidentified class '1854' 0-6-0ST in 1924 at Yealmpton waiting to leave for Plymstock. The layout of the terminus is interesting as it was designed as a through station when the extension to Modbury was proposed.   *Lens of Sutton*

The upper view looking east, shows a class '1076' 0-6-0PT on the daily goods train in the summer of 1933. The entrance to the goods yard was up under the road bridge in the distance and then reversing into a five-siding yard. The lower view shows one of the intermediate stations on the branch, Brixton Road which was 6 miles 43 chains from Plymouth. This appears to have been the only station to have had the station awning painted in two colours similar to stations on the Kingsbridge branch. Although originally established with a station master, by 1925 it had only a porter looking after it. There was a two-road goods yard at the southern end, initially controlled by a signal box but later by a ground frame. *R.W. Kidner and Lens of Sutton*

Horrabridge, on the Launceston branch, opened in June 1859 and was heralded in many GWR publications of the time as 'attractive and beautifully situated'. It had two platforms, goods shed and loading dock with the signal box (of Saxby & Farmer design) situated on the up platform. With the wide gap between the tracks, a water column was situated at either end of the station. This view in 1916 shows a GWR '3521' class 4-4-0 No. 3531, arriving with an up train for Plymouth.

Author's Collection

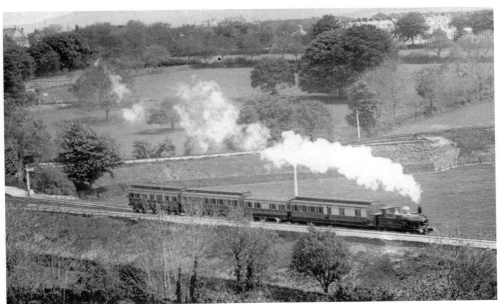

Yelverton, opened in 1885, was the junction station on the Launceston branch for Princetown which opened in 1883 (until 1885 Princetown trains ran to and from Horrabridge). In this 1905 view an unidentified 2-4-0T hauls a train towards Plymouth, with the Princetown branch in the background. *Photomatic*

The station site at Yelverton being fairly constricted, Princetown trains had no run-round loop and, after passengers detrained, the locomotive pushed its coaches out of the platform on to the branch, was then shunted into a short siding and the coaches then gravitated on their own back to the branch platform. *Lens of Sutton*

The station at Princetown, opened in August 1883, was recorded as the highest station in England at 1,373 feet above sea level and although only about 6 miles from Yelverton it took the branch train over 10½ miles of twisting, heavily graded track to reach it! This view in June 1926 shows a 2-6-2T, No. 4403 running around its train prior to its return to Yelverton. This bleak station enjoyed a goods shed, locomotive shed and turntable all controlled by a 14-lever signal box.   *H.C. Casserley*

The only intermediate station on the branch was Dousland (about 1½ miles from Yelverton) and this was built on a curve with goods shed facilities (there were three other halts provided along the branch). This early view shows permanent way staff posing with the station staff for some occasion.   *Lens of Sutton*

The 8¾ branch to Looe was built by the Liskeard and Looe Railway and leased to the GWR in 1909, but ownership did not pass to the GWR until Grouping in 1923. The line is still operating today, with a good service and four intermediate halts for the visitors to alight and walk to the various attractions of the area. The branch platform at Liskeard is at right angles to the main line and on a very steep gradient (1 in 34), the line spirals down to Coombe Jn where trains have to reverse before proceeding to Looe. The top view shows Looe station with the branch train on 23rd May, 1935 whilst the lower is a commercial postcard and shows the station on the extreme left, the corrugated carriage shed in the middle, with the small engine shed in the front. The original line continued some way along the quay with various unloading points for boats.

H.C. Casserley and Author's Collection

Station staff line up for their photograph to be taken alongside the engine of the branch train in this early view at Bodmin General. The branch connected with the GW main line at Bodmin Road. The line to Bodmin Road curved away to the left as the train left the station, curving away to the right was a GWR line linking with the LSWR's line (from a separate station in Bodmin) to Wadebridge and Padstow. The GWR branch's passenger service survived until 30th January, 1967, with goods facilities being withdrawn at Bodmin a little later, on 1st May, 1967.

As an illustration of the facilities at a station this official (June 1925) picture of Bodmin can hardly be bettered. Branch trains from Bodmin Road (on the main line to Penzance) entered the station under the bridge on which the photographer is standing, ran into the dead-end station, the engine ran-round and then the trains continued its journey to Wadebridge by the line leaving at bottom left. A lot of lever-pulling for the signalman for each train! Visible are the engine shed up against the cutting wall (*left*) and a large good shed opposite the passenger platform in the middle distance.

These two rare commercial postcards show clearly the Newquay Harbour Railway in Cornwall which was fed from a spur at Newquay GWR station. This spur, which was closed in 1926, ran from the harbour up an incline of 1 in 4½ through a solid rock tunnel, it then zig-zagged up to the top of the hill, crossing a (210 yds long and 98 ft high) timber viaduct over the Trenance Valley before reaching Newquay station. The incline was worked by wire ropes from a stationary engine and all wagons were moved around the harbour by horses. The lower view clearly shows the tunnel mouth, whilst the upper view illustrates the track layout. Apparently at the turn of the century this spur was heavily used when many ships docked in the harbour.

Author's Collection

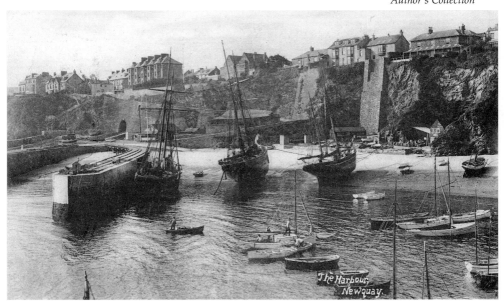

The branch from Truro to Falmouth is 11¾ miles long and was opened in August 1863 as a broad gauge line. Here a 4-4-0 is seen arriving at the terminus at the turn of the century. The line still survives today but the eight original timber viaducts have all been replaced by masonry viaducts.
Lens of Sutton

This view of Falmouth in 1895 does not show much of the station area but does at least give an impression of the shipbuilding industry that the railway served here. Note that although the track is now standard gauge, it is all laid on longitudinal timber baulks as it was when broad gauge.
LGRP

A truly GWR scene at Redruth in 1910 with bus No. 66 obviously attracting much attention. Behind is a steam railmotor providing a connecting service at Redruth which was the terminus until the line was extended to Penzance and Truro in 1852 and a new station built nearer to the town. This bus service connected the surrounding area between Redruth and Falmouth and would have been useful for passengers living west of Redruth, avoiding a long detour to Truro.
Lens of Sutton

The branch from Gwinear Road to Helston in Cornwall was opened in May 1887 as a standard gauge line and absorbed into the GWR in 1898, finally being closed to passengers in October 1964. The terminus at Helston was 8¾ miles from the junction and had a goods shed as well as a locomotive shed and carriage shed. The line was due to extend to The Lizard, but the advent of the motor-bus put paid to that idea and in fact the service from Helston to The Lizard was the first railway bus service ever, introduced on 17th August, 1903.
Lens of Sutton

Carbis Bay, an intermediate station on the St Ives branch was a very unusual station with all the main buildings high-up on a bank above the single platform, with a walkway down to the platform which provided shelter in bad weather with a brick shelter and canopy. In 1932, ten weekday trains stopped in either direction with two of them providing a through service to Penzance.
Lens of Sutton

Lelant station was the other intermediate station on the branch and this view in the early 1930s captures the station master and his dog posing in a slack period between trains. The station building had an unusual booking office, which also contained a store and the usual toilet facilities. The small building on the right contained the ground frame for access to the spur siding that served Lelant Quay.
Lens of Sutton

The beautiful station of St Ives in Cornwall is the terminus of one of the most scenic GWR branch lines. Being 4¾ miles from its junction with the main line at St Erth, it was originally built by the West Cornwall Railway and then absorbed by the GWR in August 1878. This branch terminus was built on a graceful curve, nestling into the hillside along the shore and has tempted many a railway modeller, fitting nicely into a corner position of any room. Before World War II the branch enjoyed eight trains (each way) on a Sunday, with considerable traffic during weekdays. The goods shed was adjacent to the station whilst the engine shed was down the line separated by a viaduct. Today the branch still offers travellers the chance to get away from it all. Cornwall County Council offer motorists a special all-in parking and passenger ticket to leave their cars at Lelant Saltings and travel by train into St Ives, so avoiding all the traffic jams.

Photomatic and Lens of Sutton

Railway Station. Portishead. 599.

This busy 1920s scene shows the enormous importance of the 11½ mile Bristol to Portishead branch, which the GWR absorbed in 1884. The original station seen here on the right was resited in January 1954 as a result of the construction of a power station. So busy was this line in the 1930s that the GWR had to introduce an hourly service for the branch. The line had a rail connection with the nearby Weston, Clevedon and Portishead Light Railway for 33 years from 1907. The dock sidings on the left featured a goods shed and engine shed with a turntable.

Lens of Sutton

The same scene viewed from the other direction, April 1930. A poor photograph but worthy of inclusion because it shows the station buildings in detail.

Brunel University: Mowat/Locomotive Collection

A steam railmotor No. 58 arrives with a train for Bristol at Pill, an intermediate station with a crossing loop, on the single line Portishead branch *c*. 1910.   *Lens of Sutton*

Clevedon was the terminus of a 3½ mile branch from Yatton, opened by the Bristol & Exeter Railway in June 1847. Originally broad gauge, the line was converted to standard gauge in September 1879 (it had become part of the GWR in 1876). The original signal box located on the single long platform became a ground frame as early as 1917; in this 6th August, 1932 view the solitary auto-coach is just starting away from under the station's overall roof on its short journey to Yatton.   *Brunel University: Mowat/Locomotive Collection*

Blagdon station, the terminus of the 6¾ mile Wrington Vale Light Railway from Congresbury in Somerset, was depicted by GWR publicity department with the following statement: 'Tourists would be inclined to heartily thank the GWR for opening up to them a bit of Somersetshire of exceptional beauty, . . . Bristol to Blagdon for the lake and to Burrington Coome, the cleft in the rocks where the Revd Toplady compiled the hymn, 'Rock of Ages', . . . Special Day trips'. There were three intermediate stations on the branch. Blagdon station, opened on 4th December, 1901 (with no less than 1,500 passengers!), contained a run-round loop, mileage siding, loading dock and originally an engine shed. The upper view shows an 0-4-2T on a rake of four-wheeled coaches, which were equipped with low alighting boards to cope with very low platforms on the branch. The passenger service ceased on 14th September, 1931. The lower view shows the whole of the station with the Bristol Waterworks Co. buildings dominating the skyline; these served the Yeo reservoir nearby. The pumping station had its own private siding from 1904-1941. A camping coach based at the station proved very popular with those seeking to fish the reservoir for trout. The branch engine can be seen in the background and was a 2-4-0ST, No. 1384, with four-wheeled stock when this photograph was taken.

Photomatic and Author's Collection

Wrington, a simple intermediate station on the branch, had just one siding on which the solitary truck is standing. The section from Wrington to Blagdon (3¾ miles) closed completely in November 1950, track being removed between 1952 and 1954, but Congresbury to Wrington (2¾ miles) remained open for freight until June 1963, track being removed in 1964. This picture is *c.* 1930, before closure to passengers.   *Brunel University: Mowat/Locomotive Collection*

Dunkerton was an intermediate station on the Camerton branch between Hallatrow and Limpley Stoke, a branch best remembered for the comedy film *The Titfield Thunderbolt* which was filmed on it after closure. The branch opened in stages, Hallatrow-Camerton in March 1882, Camerton-Dunkerton Colliery in August 1907, and Dunkerton Colliery-Limpley Stoke (on which section Dunkerton was located) in May 1910. This picture was probably taken on or about the date of opening because everything is in pristine condition. The passenger service was withdrawn as a wartime economy on 22nd March, 1915 and not restored until 9th July, 1923, but only lasted until 21st September, 1925. After this date Hallatrow to Camerton was little used and most of the track in this section was lifted in 1932. Dunkerton box closed on 19th November, 1925 (having been closed also between 1918 and July 1923), the crossing loop and siding all being disused from this date. The section from Camerton to Limpley Stoke survived until 15th February, 1951 mainly for the benefit of Camerton Colliery which closed in 1950.   *British Rail*

The stations on the GW/Midland Joint line between Ashley Hill Jn and Avonmouth Dock. (*Top*) Clifton Down station opened on 1st October, 1874 and was the terminus for several years; freight trains continued on to Avonmouth from February 1877 but the line was not made suitable for passenger trains until 1885. Avonmouth Dock station (*bottom*) opened on 1st September, 1885. The original island platform (*right*) was extended in 1917 and a new up platform (*left*) opened in 1918. Both stations remain open today. *(Both) Brunel University: Mowat/Locomotive Collection*

The Golden Valley line ran from Pontrilas to Hay in Herefordshire and was opened by the GWR in May 1901, after they acquired it in 1899, when the line had become bankrupt just after completion. Here the top view shows the main line station at Pontrilas in the late 1930s with a through train *en route* to Newport. The branch train can just be seen standing in the bay platform on the left.   *R.W. Kidner Collection*

The lower view shows a branch line service with class '517' class 0-4-2T No. 1437 in charge of three 4-wheeled coaches and an iron mink. The service was very poor and the passenger facilities were withdrawn very early in 1941. It took well over the hour for the trains to complete the 18 mile trip!   *R.W. Kidner Collection*

The next station down the branch was Abbeydore which opened in September 1881 and closed to passenger traffic in December 1941. The station building was of timber and designed by the Gloucester Carriage & Wagon Co. This and other stations on the line mainly depended on pick-up goods traffic and timber. This view in the late 1930s shows the station building which housed (*left to right*): lamp room, general office, waiting room, ladies' room and toilets. The loop, which left the running line just after the level crossing, served a cattle loading dock and pens.

Lens of Sutton

Following Abbeydore came Bacton. First shown in the 1st July, 1903 timetable, it was previously referred to as Bacton Road and as this view shows it was a very basic station for passengers, however it did have a station master living on site. The crossing gates and loop just behind the crossing were controlled by a ground frame.

Lens of Sutton

Peterchurch came next, just 7¾ miles from Pontrilas and was the site of the 'cutting of the first sod' for the Golden Valley line on 31st August, 1876. The station had only one short platform with a passing loop and a headshunt into a cattle dock, on the Hay side of the station. Seen here in an Edwardian summer view, with a class '517' 0-4-2T approaching hauling a train of six-wheelers. Although closed to passengers in 1941, freight services ran on until 1953.

Lens of Sutton

In this 1930s view is Dorstone (10½ miles) which was the only station on the line to have two platforms, even though they were staggered; the intention was to allow for two passenger trains to run, however, one engine in steam was employed on this branch and it appears that the second platform was never used.

R.H. Clark Collection

Finally, the last station to be portrayed on this picturesque line is Westbrook, seen here in 1931. Although a rather gloomy picture, the neat and attractive nature of this rural retreat is evident. In 1932 the station was served by only two trains each way, with a third on Thursdays only.

Brunel University: Mowat/Locomotive Collection

The Leominster and Kington Railway opened to Kington on 27th July, 1857, public traffic commencing on 20th August. A separate company the Kington & Eardisley Railway was authorised to build a railway between these two places in June 1862, but it took until August 1874 for the 6¾ mile line to be constructed. This railway enjoyed running powers over the Leominster line for the 1¼ miles to Titley, the actual junction for Eardisley. Expansion now came thick and fast in this very rural area: the Leominster line was extended from Kington to New Radnor on 25th September, 1875 which involved a new, through station at Kington, actually built by the Eardisley company and becoming joint property. Finally the Leominster & Kington Railway built a line from Titley to Presteign, 5¾ miles long, which opened just before the New Radnor extension on 9th September, 1875. Below we see a busy animated scene at the first station out of Leominster towards Kington, Kingsland, at an unknown date but during the period when railways played an important part in life in the rural community.

R.H. Clark Collection

This view shows Kington, looking towards Titley, the signal box can just be seen at the end of the up platform, the main station buildings being on the downside. Beyond and to the right of the massive goods shed was the site of the first passenger station.   *Lens of Sutton*

Kington downside station buildings (*right*), goods shed (*centre*) and goods yard, looking towards the first passenger station (closed in 1875), the old station building can be seen left of the goods shed; again photographed on 12th August, 1932.

Brunel University: Mowat/Locomotive Collection

The old passenger station at Kington looking from the buffer-stops towards the goods yard on 12th August, 1932, showing clearly the cattle pens just to the right of the old station building. The extension of the branch to New Radnor closed between New Radnor and Dolyhir on 31st December, 1951 and between Dolyhir and Kington on 9th June, 1958; Kington to Leominster closed on 28th September, 1964. The Eardisley branch closed in October 1940.

Brunel University: Mowat/Locomotive Collection

The Presteign branch ran from Titley parallel to the New Radnor to Leominster line for about a mile before curving away. The line had one intermediate halt opened on 9th March, 1929 called Forge Crossing. The view below captures the scene in 1910 with a Swindon class 0-6-0ST arriving at Presteign from Kington. The train comprises four-wheel coaches and a GWR Toad brake van.

Lens of Sutton

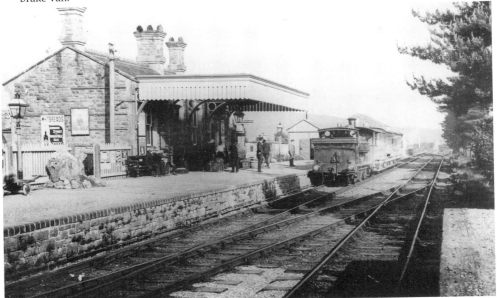

Presteign, the terminus of the 5¾ mile branch from Titley. Opened on 9th September, 1875, it was worked from the outset by the GWR. Trains actually worked to and from Kington, 1¾ miles west of Titley in the direction of New Radnor and the train set was shared between Presteign and Eardisely branches; in 1932 there were three trains each way on each branch, weekdays only. The branch closed to passengers on 5th February, 1951 but freight lingered on until 28th September, 1964. This 1914 view shows a two-coach train of four-wheeled stock headed by a '1701' class 0-6-0ST.
Lens of Sutton

An Armstrong '517' class 0-4-2T, No. 525, stands at the head of the Kington service at Presteign c. 1906.
Lens of Sutton

Pencader was the junction for Newcastle Emlyn and was reached by the broad gauge Carmarthen & Cardigan Railway on 28th March, 1864, but the Board of Trade objected to the use of the station because of the severe gradient on which it was built; trains ran to Llandyssul, the first station (3½ miles) towards Newcastle Emlyn from 3rd June, 1864. The standard gauge Manchester & Milford Railway (M&M) reached Pencader from the north, the 12¼ miles from Lampeter to Pencader, being opened on 1st January, 1866. Once mixed gauge had been laid south of Pencader, M&M trains were able to run through to Carmarthen from 1st November, 1866. The M&M was extended from Lampeter to Strata Florida on 1st September, 1866 and to Aberystwyth on 12th August, 1867; it got no nearer to Manchester (nor Milford for that matter)! Llandyssul to Newcastle Emlyn was not built until 1st July, 1895 and closed to passengers as early as 15th September, 1952. The top picture shows a busy scene at Pencader with trains crossing; notice how the platform supporting wall has had to be shored up. In the bottom picture (all?) the staff at Newcastle Emlyn line up for a photograph sometime in the short life of the rural terminus. By the look of the cycle on the platform it would appear to be 1920s or 1930s.
Lens of Sutton and HMRS

Lampeter was the junction for the Aberayron branch which opened as late as 10th April, 1911 (freight) and 12th May, 1911 (passengers). Not surprisingly, in view of the rural nature of this part of Wales branch passenger trains were withdrawn on 10th February, 1951, but milk traffic to Felin Fach, midway along the branch, continued until 1st October, 1973. Aberystwyth to Strata Florida closed, following flooding, on 14th December, 1964 and the remainder of the Manchester & Milford line to Carmarthen closed to passengers on 22nd February, 1965. Lampeter remained open for freight traffic until 1st October, 1973. Here in more prosperous times, is a scene at Lampeter on a 'Horse Fair' day, probably in the first 20 years of this century.

British Rail

The GWR inherited the Mawddwy Railway from the Cambrian in 1922 and it ran until July 1951 for freight, with the passenger service being withdrawn on 1st January, 1931. Here at Cemmes Road in 1927, GWR 2-4-0 No. 1329 is being prepared for its trip up the 6¾ mile branch to Dinas Mawddwy (passing through three intermediate stations) hauling four-wheeled coaching stock.

J.S. Kite

The Kerry branch (3¼ miles) opened in March 1863, was absorbed by the Cambrian in 1864 and came into GWR ownership on 25th March, 1922. Here 0-6-0T No. 26 (Cambrian Railways) shunts at Abermule in 1920 assembling the train for the trip to Kerry. The line had two small halts along the way. *Roger Carpenter Collection*

Blaenau Festiniog GWR station, the terminus of the lengthy branch from Bala, pictured in 1912. Initially the 3 mile section south from Blaenau Festiniog to Festiniog was built by the Festiniog & Blaenau Railway, of 1 ft 11½in. gauge and was worked practically as a branch of the narrow gauge Festiniog Railway (which is seen on the left); it opened on 29th May, 1868. The Bala & Festiniog Railway, standard gauge and whose Chairman was Sir Daniel Gooch, Chairman of the GWR, reached Llan Festiniog on 1st November, 1882 and Blaenau Festiniog on 10th September, 1883 after the narrow gauge Festiniog & Blaenau Railway was converted to standard gauge. After plans were put forward for a new reservoir in the Treweryn Valley in 1957, it was decided to close the line rather than divert it and passenger closure came on 2nd January, 1960 and freight on 27th January, 1961. In the meantime, however, a new nuclear power station was built at Trawsfynydd, some 6½ miles south of Blaenau Festiniog, and a new connection installed (on 20th April, 1964) between the former GWR branch and the former LNWR branch at Blaenau Festiniog to allow traffic to run via Llandudno Jn, over the Conway Valley route and what remained of the former GWR Bala branch to the new facility.   *British Rail*

The halt of Berwig was on the Wrexham to Minera branch and opened on 1st May, 1905 and was the last station on the line, which then carried on to the Minera Lime works. The line, in its heyday around 1910, had 14 workings a day and four extra ones on Saturdays mainly catering for miners and steelworkers.   *Lens of Sutton*

Llangollen was close to the beginning of the secondary main line from Ruabon to Dolgelley and was opened by the Vale of Llangollen Railway (worked by the GWR) on 1st December, 1861 (goods) and 2nd June, 1862 (passenger). Originally single track, the line between Ruabon and Llangollen was doubled in 1898. The line closed to passengers on 18th January, 1965 and to freight on 1st April, 1968. The still intact station is now headquarters of the Llangollen Railway Society.   *E.R. Morten*

Tenbury Wells station in Herefordshire was the last station of the GWR section of the Bewdley to Woofferton line and opened in August 1864. There were two sections of this branch with Tenbury being in the middle: the Tenbury Railway from Woofferton to Tenbury and the Tenbury & Bewdley Railway absorbed by the GWR in 1869. Here a '517' class 0-4-2T enters with a train from Bewdley. The cattle dock in the foreground had just been built in this 1913 view; the small extension to the station buildings was a ladies' waiting room. On the extreme left was the signal box situated on the up platform alongside the waiting rooms and on the right, a brick-built goods shed.

Lens of Sutton

Stourbridge Town in 1947, just prior to nationalisation with 0-4-2T No. 1414 attached to auto-trailer No. 76. This was the GWR's shortest branch, only ¾ mile from Stourbridge Junction; opened in 1879 for passengers, a second line was opened for goods in 1880 (the two tracks running parallel and giving the appearance of a double track), the branch is still operating today. The freight branch continued past the station into a huge canal basin (17 sidings to hold 168 wagons) which had a massive two-road goods shed. Lines were laid right along the canal bank to facilitate rail/canal 'quick' loading. Even further was a complex of private sidings alongside the River Stour. The lower view shows pannier tank No. 2711 on a main line train of clerestory stock bound for Birmingham at Stourbridge Junction.   *H.C. Casserley and Lens of Sutton*

The 9 mile branch from Moreton-in-Marsh to Shipston-on-Stour was shown in the 1938 GWR Working Timetable as a tramway and was opened as standard gauge in July 1889, having been converted from an earlier horse-drawn tramway to Stratford-upon-Avon. The passenger service was withdrawn early in 1929 (if there were many), being replaced by a motor-bus, however freight continued on the branch until May 1960. The intermediate station of Stretton-on-Fosse boasted a station master (seen here with his son and dog, in between the rare train movements!). The siding was controlled by a nearby ground frame and the 'complex' had a weighbridge and office. Note the unusual station nameboard, replaced later by the standard GWR board in the next picture.

Lens of Sutton

A later view of Stretton-on-Fosse looking towards the crossing gates. The double gates on the right give access to the limited goods facilities at the station. *Lens of Sutton*

The other intermediate station on the branch was Longden Road, and was, from 1889, the site of a triangular junction between the original horse-drawn tramway from Moreton-in-Marsh which continued northwards from here to Stratford-upon-Avon and a new construction eastwards to Shipston-on-Stour, built by the GWR. Goods traffic for Stratford was worked via the goods yard at Longden Road, but the old tramway was last used in 1904. *Lens of Sutton*

Great Alne was situated on a GWR line between Alcester (on the LMS branch between Redditch and Ashchurch) and Bearley on the GWR line from Stratford-upon-Avon to Hatton. Like several other short lines, the Alcester branch closed in 1917 during World War I and the rails were removed for the steel, the line not reopening until 18th December, 1922, between Bearley and Great Alne only. The section onwards to Alcester was restored on 1st August, 1923, but the branch only survived until 1st March, 1951. At Great Alne, seen here on 13th June, 1934, there was a single goods siding, access being controlled by a ground frame at each end. Just over two miles away, towards Bearley, a halt at Aston Cantlow comprised the only other revenue-earning potential on this short branch.

Brunel University: Mowat/Locomotive Collection